GRAYCE MAYHEW

Your Guide to Madrid

When You Only Have One Day

D1738539

First edition

This book was professionally typeset on Reedsy.
Find out more at reedsy.com

Contents

1

Chapter 1

Introduction

Welcome to one day of getting acquainted with Madrid! It's both a historic and a modern city. Once you start looking around this beautiful and lively capital city I hope you fall in love with it and its people, as I have, and return when you can take more time to truly savor all it has to offer.

2

Chapter 2

Historical Overview

Madrid, called Mayarit in Arabic, was first documented around 852, though it was inhabited long before that. It was under the control of the Muslims who ruled much of Southern Spain from 711 to 1492.It was a military outpost with a fortress surrounded by walls. Some areas of the wall can still be seen. Christians conquered this small outpost around 1083. It wasn't until 1561 when King Philip II moved his court from the former capital of Toledo to Madrid that it developed into an important government center. As it grew the population became more diverse: there were the original Muslim inhabitants, settlers from Castile and Leon (Christians), some Franks, and a smaller Jewish community. It was mainly agricultural, but there were two notable enterprises: building materials manufacturing and leather goods.

It grew rapidly in the 1600s, attracting many leading Spanish artists and writers, a time known as the Golden Century (Siglo de Oro). In the 1700s, under Charles III (1716–1788), many buildings we see today were erected: Royal Palace, Prado Museum, Alcala Gate. The Hapsburg family (from Austria) ruled; then the Bourbon family (France) came to power. In 1808 Napoleon invaded Madrid and Spain was under French rule until 1814 when King Ferdinand VII returned to the throne. Alfonse XIII, last king in the early 20th century, had the Gran Via constructed. With the Second Republic (1931-39) the Casa de Campo became a public park (before that it was exclusive to the royalty's use). The Spanish Civil War 1936-39 was a precursor of World War II. In 1939 General Franciso Franco came to power and remained so until reinstalling the monarchy with King Juan Carlos Bourbon in 1975. Juan Carlos' son Philip VI is Spain's current king.

From 1948-1954 Madrid grew by annexing surrounding municipalities. In the 1980s Madrid consolidated its position as the leading economic, cultural, industrial, educational and technological center. It experienced economic difficulties in 2008 and more recently with the COVID pandemic. Since then many areas have improved, especially tourism.

Chapter 3

Pre-Planning

Documents

US citizens need to have a valid passport to travel to Spain and can stay up to 90 days without a visa. Starting in 2025, US citizens may need a Spain ETIAS (Travel Authorization) to travel to Spain. The ETIAS is valid for three years and can be applied for online.

Going by Air

Check with your favorite travel websites to see what flights are available, their costs and conditions.Major carriers fly there, and Spain's airline is Iberia. You may find special offers. Suggestions: **https://www.expedia.com/** or **https://www.iberia.com/**

Travel Insurance

If this is your first overseas flight, continue reading.If you're an experienced traveler, skip this section.

Three of the most important coverages are: Trip Cancellation and Trip Interruption, Travel Delay Coverage, and Medical Coverage and Medical Evacuation Coverage.

You have several choices of companies or you may include it when you purchase your ticket or trip package. Some companies are AIG Travel Guard, AXA, and Allianz. Review what you choose to be sure you're getting what you want and need. Note the customer support numbers and hours. You can take a picture on your phone and write out and carry the information with you as a backup.

Airport Transfer to Hotels

You may want to reserve private transportation from the airport directly to your hotel as it can save you time. Here are three suggestions:

https://www.tripadvisor.com/AttractionProductReview-g187514-d16823014-Madrid_Barajas_Airport_Private_Transfer_To_Madrid_City-Madrid.html

For a private vehicle, prices are from $32.16 US per adult and vary based on group size.Make your reservation and then pay either when your plans are set or let auto-pay do it two days before you travel.

https://madridairporttaxis.com/ Book before you go and pay the driver in cash when you get to your hotel. Prices vary.See website for details.

https://www.suntransfers.com/madrid-airport From$37.83 US for up to 4 adults; prices vary; excellent reviews on tripadvisor. See website for details.

Other options are in the Arrival and Getting Settled section.

When to Go

Spring (March–May): With average daily highs between 59°F to 68°F, it's a great time to be outdoors; there are lots of activities. May is not the peak season, and there is usually good weather.

Summer: Madrid has hot summer days (highs can be above 100°F), various festivals, and many residents are out of town on vacation. This time coincides with school vacations, so many people come.

Fall (September–November): This is an ideal time of year. Temperatures are still warm but without being too hot or humid. It's mostly sunny.

Winter (November–February): This can be the least expensive time to visit; weather is usually dry and sunny. On the other hand, temperatures can drop below 50°F. On my most recent visit in January it rained.Snow can occur. In December and January there are many Christmas markets and lights; including the parade of the three Wise Men on January 5th. (They take the place of Santa Claus and bring children gifts that night.)

What to Pack

Depending on the time of year and what you plan to do, pack shorts and shirts or long sleeved tops and pants. You may want to include a "dress up" outfit for a club or special event; otherwise, casual dress works well, especially for students. Most *madrileños* are very stylish, but you need to be comfortable. Be sure you take a sturdy pair of walking shoes. You may also want to purchase some euros in advance of your trip. You can easily buy them upon arrival at Madrid's airport.

Chapter 4

Starting Your Trip

Arriving and Getting Settled

Madrid's airport is located in Barajas, just outside the city. Once you arrive, you can change money into euros at one of the exchange counters in the airport or use one of the ATM machines. You may have also purchased euros in the US beforehand. Once you've cleared customs and retrieved your luggage (terminal 4 or T4), you have several options to get to the city:

- Taxi or Uber: look for a taxi stand or check out Uber to take you directly to your hotel or other lodging. Uber is also called Cabify in Spain. City taxis are white with a red stripe. It's a fixed fare to the city center: 30 euros ($32.65 US); for some areas it's 40 euros ($43.54 US) Please tip 10%; more if you have extra special service. Travel time is 30-45 minutes, depending on your destination and traffic.

- Airport Express: express bus from Terminals 4, 2 and 1 to Plaza de Cibeles and Atocha (train station); look for wide yellow stripe along the length of the bus; runs 24 hours and costs 5 euros ($5.45 US); pay on the bus: tap your phone or credit card, or use cash; takes about 30 minutes, depending on traffic. Once you're at Plaza de Cibeles, check your hotel's address. If it's along the Gran Vía or near Plaza de España you can take city bus line 2 and get off at the stop nearest your hotel. If your hotel is near Puerta del Sol, you can take the same bus and get off at Gran Vía-Montera stop. Walk down Montera to Sol. If the Express shuttle takes you to Atocha Station, look for the Metro sign and take line 1 to Sol or Gran Vía stations. See above directions to continue.

- Metro (subway): Line 8 (Rosa) connects the airport to the city center, with stations in terminals 2 and 4. The trip takes about 30−40 minutes, and tickets cost around 5 euros. The metro runs from 6:05 AM−1:33 AM, with more frequent service during the day. At Nuevos Ministerios Station, you can transfer to Line 10 and go to Plaza de España. To get to Sol, take Line 10 to Tribunal and change to Line 1 to Sol.

- Bus: Buses run every 15 minutes during the day and every 35 minutes at night, and the trip takes about 40 minutes. Tickets cost 5 euros and can be purchased on the bus. Buses stop at terminals T1, T2, and T4, but traffic may make the trip longer than the metro.

- Train: Two suburban RENFE (Spain's train system) lines, C1 and C10, depart from the airport train station in T4 and connect the airport to many areas of Madrid. You can probably get to the city center in about 45 minutes.

- See the Places to Stay section for directions to 4 hotel examples.

Places to Stay

The places listed here are near the center city and shown from lowest to highest cost. They are within walking distance to various sites, restaurants, bars, and more. When giving telephone numbers, I've included Spain's country code 34. Depending on your phone, you may not need it. The next number is 91, the city code or 685 for cell phones. You'll also see the directions from the airport. Check websites to see what amenities are important to you. You can compare places through www.booking.com , **https://www.expedia.com/** , or your preferred site. *Note: street addresses have the street name first and then the number.*

Hotel Mirador Puerta del Sol

Located at Calle de la Montera 7; cost: under $100 US per person per night; tel: (+34) 910 32 53 64. It's a small place with 22 rooms. Mirador means a look out. From windows in this hotel you can see parts of Sol; see website for amenities and other details: www.miradorpuertadelsol.com The street connects Puerta del Sol at one end with Gran Vía at the other.

From the airport, you can have several options:

- a prearranged private car
- a city taxi,
- Airport Express bus to Cibeles then city bus line 2 to GranVía-Montera stop, walk down Montera to #7,
- Metro Line 8 from airport to Nuevos Ministerios, Line 10 to Tribunal and Line 1 to Sol; walk up Montera to #7
- Airport Express bus to Atocha Train Station,find the Metro sign and take line 1 to Sol; walk up Montera to #7.

Hotel Mayerling Madrid

Located at Calle del Conde Romanones 6; about 1700 feet from both Puerta del Sol and Plaza Mayor; cost: about $100 US per person per night; tel: (+34) 914 20 15 80; part of a chain; see website for amenities and other details: https://www.mayerlinghotel.com/en (the en means info is in English); if you book on their website, there's a discount. From the airport, you can choose:

· pre-arranged private car,
· city taxi,
· Airport Express bus to Cibeles then city bus line 2 to GranVía-Montera stop, walk down Montera to Sol, take Calle Carretas to Plaza Jacinto Benavente, then Calle de Concepción Jerónima, first left is Calle del Conde Romanones,
· Metro Line 8 from airport to Nuevos Ministerios, Line 10 to Tribunal and Line 1 to Sol, then take Calle Carretas to Plaza Jacinto Benavente, then Calle de Concepción Jerónima, first left is Calle del Conde Romanones
· Airport Express bus to Atocha Train Station,find the Metro sign and take line 1 to Sol, take Calle Carretas to Plaza Jacinto Benavente, then Calle de Concepción Jerónima, first left is Calle del Conde Romanones.

Oriente Palace Apartments

Located at Calle de Lepanto 6 close to the Royal Palace and Plaza del Oriente (as the name implies); cost: around $120-140 US per person per night; tel:(+34) 685 87 55 62; see website for amenities and other details: https://www.orientepalace.com/index_EN (the EN means info is in English)

From the airport are the same basic options:

- pre-arranged private car,
- city taxi,
- Metro Line 8 from airport to Nuevos Ministerios, Line 10 to Alonso Martinez, and Line 5 to Opera, then about 220 yards going toward Plaza de Oriente is Calle de Lepanto.

Riu Plaza España

Located at Gran Vía 84 in the Edificio España (Spain Building); one of the tower building on Plaza de España; cost: from $195 US per person per night; tel:(+34) 919 19 33 93; one of many Riu hotels round the world; see website for amenities, other details and to make a reservation: https·//w ww.riu.com/en/hotel/spain/madrid/hotel-riu-plaza-espana/ (the en means info is in English)

From the airport: pre-arranged private car or city taxi.With what you're spending to stay at this luxury hotel, you probably won't look at other options. Be sure to take advantage of all this amazing hotel has to offer, including restaurants and great views from the various terrace levels.

5

Chapter 5

Getting Around

Public transportation: bus, metro (subway) and taxi

Public transportation is excellent and inexpensive. You can purchase tickets at subway entrances and on the buses, get a multi-ride ticket or even a tourist pass. Here's a helpful website with public transportation information and much more: https://www.esmadrid.com/en (the en means info is in English)

Within that website is an area that explains in English all about the tourist travel pass: what it is, why you would want one, where you can use it, and what it costs.It's possible to save money even for one day: https://www.esmadrid.com/en/madrid-tourist-travel-pass ©
MADRID DESTINO CULTURA TURISMO Y NEGOCIO S. A. MADRID DESTINO CULTURA TURISMO Y NEGOCIO S. A.

Special note: There are two regular city buses with circular routes: C1 and C2. If you use both, you'll make a circle of many neighborhoods. The end points are Glorieta Cuatro Caminos (north) and Glorieta Embajadores (south). The cost is 1.50 euros(about $1.65 US) and each half takes about an hour. You can find some of the stops for C2 near the Sabatini Gardens by the Royal Palace and around the Plaza de España, which are shown later on in this guide.

Sight-seeing buses

Check out some of the agencies offering tours: Viator, Big Bus Tours, Madrid City Tour or Trip Advisor. You can hop on or off at all their stops. Prices range from $27 US on up, depending on which type of tour you want: Historical Madrid or Modern Madrid. The Madrid City Tour's main address is Calle Felipe IV and phone: (34) 933 17 64 54.You can purchase tickets online or wherever you hop on their buses. Stops are all along Gran Vía, for example.

6

Chapter 6

Deciding What to See

What you decide to see depends on your interests. Are you looking for historical places, including museums? Would you prefer to be outdoors most of the day at parks, gardens, and monuments? Madrid offers all of these options. You can get a good overview by taking one of the city bus tours mentioned in the previous section.They include a map you can use later. Be sure to leave time to enjoy tapas, chocolate con churros, some restaurant's specialties, shopping, and maybe a flamenco show or night club dancing.They're all included in upcoming chapters. By the way, tapas are in several countries now, not just in Spain.If you haven't heard of them, they are like appetizers accompanied by a small glass of draft beer or house wine.Many places have their specialties, and you can go bar hopping, tasting one or two tapas at each stop. (Prices are less if you stand at the bar rather than sitting at a table.)

Using the hotels under Places to Stay, we'll look at what's in each area. You may be staying at another hotel and can use the Highlights Overview chapter to create additional itineraries. Addresses are listed with the locations here; descriptions are in the Highlights Overview chapter. Hotel Mirador Puerta del Sol, located at Calle de la Montera 7, is a few steps from the Puerta del Sol. At Sol:

- Say hello to the bear-with-the tree statue (a symbol of Madrid)
- Stand on the zero kilometer that marks the beginning of Spain's major highways
- Treat yourself to a sweet delight at the Mallorquina at one end
- Check out the Apple store at the other end
- Take the street Carrera de San Jerónimo (by the Apple store) to Paseo del Prado (about 8 blocks) and cross all the way over to the Prado Museum; enjoy the audio tour and the many great artists
- Cross back over Paseo del Prado going toward Atocha Station (southish); cross Calle de Atocha and Calle Santa Isabel to the Reina Sofía Museum at number 52.In its contemporary collection is Picasso's famous Guernica, depicting the horrors of a bombing. (More details are in the Highlights Overview)
- Go back along Paseo del Prado to number 8, the Thyssen-Bornemisza Museum, with over 1000 works of art from the 1300s through the more recent movements
- Head back across Paseo del Prado once more and go up the hill behind the Prado to Retiro Park, with many entrances and activities; entrance is free; some activities are not
- Exit Retiro on Calle de Alcalá at Plaza de la Independencia to view the Puerta de Alcalá or Alcalá Gate Monument; centuries past it was an entrance to the city
- Continue downhill on Calle de Alcalá to Plaza de Cibeles to catch the goddess on her chariot pulled by lions, noting the architecture of the cathedral-like building that was the main post office and is now City Hall
- Follow Calle de Alcalá a short distance before taking a half-right

onto Gran Vía; check out the shops, theaters, cafes and restaurants until reaching Plaza de Callao

- Go through Plaza de Callao to Calle Preciados; stop in at the Galerias Preciados department store; on its top floor are several eateries and an observation deck with great city views
- Continue down Preciados to Sol, go over two streets to Montera and return to your hotel
- Otherwise, return to Gran Via and continue on to Plaza de España; pick up from where the Riu Plaza information begins in a bit.

Hotel Mayerling Madrid, located at Calle del Conde Romanones 6, is near to the Puerta del Sol and the Plaza Mayor:

- Several blocks away is the Churrería Chocolatería 1902, located at Calle de San Martín 2; famous for its *chocolate con churros*, a delicious breakfast treat any time
- Nearby do wander through the Plaza Mayor, the largest public space in Madrid where celebrations have taken place for over 400 years
- From the plaza area follow Calle Mayor to Sol and continue exploring using the information from the Hotel Mirador Puerta del Sol above
- Or from the plaza and its surroundings follow Calle Mayor in the opposite direction until reaching Calle de Bailén. Now you're at the Royal Palace, one of the largest in Europe. On one side of it are the Sabatini Gardens; on the other is the Cathedral of Santa María de la Almudena. Behind it are manicured gardens
- After visiting the Palacio Real (Royal Palace), continue on Calle Bailén past the Sabatini Gardens to the Plaza de España and pick up where the Riu Plaza information begins in a bit
- Or go in the opposite direction along Calle Bailén past Almudena Cathedral and its crypt; go right onto Calle Mayor, follow around Cuesta de la Vega on its various turns and go down steps to Calle de

Segovia; go right onto Calle de Segovia to Puente de Segovia (Segovia Bridge); at the bridge go down steps to Parque Río; reverse the route to return to the Palacio Real.

Oriente Palace Apartments, located at Calle de Lepanto 6 close to the Royal Palace and Plaza del Oriente:

· Go to the Plaza del Oriente, cross the Plaza and Calle de Bailén to Palacio Real; after visiting the Palacio Real (Royal Palace), continue on Calle Bailén past the Sabatini Gardens to the Plaza de España and pick up where the Riu Plaza information begins in a bit
· Or go in the opposite direction along Calle Bailén past Almudena Cathedral and its crypt; go right onto Calle Mayor, follow around Cuesta de la Vega on its various turns and go down steps to Calle de Segovia; go right onto Calle de Segovia to Puente de Segovia (Segovia Bridge); at the bridge go down steps to Parque Río; reverse the route to return to Palacio Real and Oriente Palace Apartments.

Riu Plaza España, located at Gran Vía 84 in the Edificio España (Spain Building); one of the tower buildings on Plaza de España, is across the street from the Plaza de España:

· Continue on Calle Bailén to the Plaza de España, one of Madrid's largest squares. Walk around and see the monument to the great Spanish author Miguel de Cervantes along with his two beloved characters: Don Quixote and his sidekick Sancho Panza. By the way Don is not a name but a title of respect
· To reach Parque del Oeste (West Park) with Egyptian temple and rose garden: go along Plaza de España street to Ferraz; cross Ferraz to the park and look for signs to Templo de Debod (Debod Temple)
· To Rosaleda (Rose Garden): go toward the Calle de la Rosaleda and

turn right; the Rosaleda is on the right after around 500 feet

- To Casa de Campo: return along Calle de la Rosaleda to junction of Paseo del Rey and Calle Irún and follow Paseo del Rey to Principe Pío; enter through RENFE; take Metro line 10 to Puerta del Sur (end of the line); exit via Lago (Lake); both the lake and the swimming pool are nearby though in opposite directions; to return to Plaza de España take subway line 10 to the Plaza de España stop

- To Faro de Moncloa: (Moncloa Lighthouse); tower location is Avenida de la Memoria 2; on the Calle Princesa by Plaza de España take bus 133 toward Moncloa; get off in 5 stops and walk the remaining distance of about 600 yards; excellent panoramic views of the city and surrounding areas; can explore the area including the university or return to Plaza de España.

7

Chapter 7

Highlights Overview

Places

Puerta del Sol

One of the most famous squares. Its clock tower chimes in each new year as everyone eats 12 grapes, one on each chime, for good luck. Beneath the tower is a symbol engraved in the sidewalk marking the beginning of the major Spanish highways called kilometer 0. Two well-known statues are the Oso y el Madroño (bear and strawberry tree) and King Carlos III on horseback. There are shops and restaurants nearby. A famous century plus old restaurant and pastry shop, the Mallorquina, is at one end and a relatively new Apple store at the other. Streets leading out of this square go to the Gran Vía, Plaza Mayor (Main Square) and the Royal Palace.

Plaza Mayor

In the heart of the city it's the largest public space in Madrid. After many years of construction, it was inaugurated in 1620, the site of many celebrations for over four centuries. An equestrian statue of King Philip III stands in its center. Just off the plaza is the oldest restaurant, Casa Botín, established in 1725. Its specialties are suckling pig and roasted lamb. You may also encounter strolling musicians in the evening. They look like troubadours from the 1500's and are known as the "Tunos", short for "estudiantina" (student). They are usually university students, and they'll serenade you from their repertoire of typical songs like *Clavelitos* (Little Carnations).

Palacio Real

The Royal Palace is a short walk from Plaza Mayor. It's the largest in Western Europe, officially the Spanish royal family's Madrid residence, but now used for state ceremonies. The site dates back to when the Muslims built their fortress, greatly expanded over the centuries and burned down in 1734. The one we see today was finished in 1755. Of note are the many historical and artistic treasures found throughout. There are also incredible royal apartments, furnishings, and galleries. Adjacent to the palace are Plaza de la Armería, Plaza del Oriente (a rectangular park connecting the palace to the Royal Theater, Sabatini Gardens (adjoining the north side of the Royal Palace and named for Francesco Sabatini who designed the royal stables that previously occupied the site, and Almudena Cathedral. Sabatini's work includes other buildings or monuments around the city. Get your tickets online in advance: https://tickets.patrimonionacional.es/en/tickets/palacio-real-de-madrid .

Almudena Cathedral

Adjacent to the Royal Palace is the Santa Maria de la Almudena cathedral, on the same site as a mosque in Muslim times, it honors Madrid's female patron saint; the name comes from the old citadel (Arabic : al-mudayna). Construction began in 1883 and finished in 1993, which resulted in many architectural styles. Admission is free to the cathedral, but donations are requested.To visit the museum, regular admission is about $8 US, with reduced prices for various groups. Hours are M-Sa 10 am-2:30 pm. It's closed on Sundays, as there are regular services. You can also visit the crypt for $3.25 US.Please remember that this cathedral is a working parish and be respectful of worshippers.

Gran Vía

It's a major thoroughfare constructed in 1924 and nicknamed the "Spanish Broadway". It goes from Calle Alcalá to Plaza de España with an abundance of hotels, movie theaters and stores. A variety of restaurants are along its central section that also leads to the Puerta del Sol.

Plaza de España

Located at the western end of the Gran Vía, this public plaza has been re-constructed with pedestrians and cyclists in mind. Regular traffic runs beneath it. Pathways connect it to the areas by the Royal Palace. The monument to Cervantes stands tall with his best-known characters of

Don Quixote and Sancho Panza. There are fountains, a playground, and many trees making this a wonderful green zone. Archaeological remains came to light during reconstruction and became part of the square to delight the public. The Tower of Madrid and the Spain Building are the two famous adjoining skyscrapers.

Moncloa Lighthouse (Faro de Moncloa)

It's a former transmission tower built in 1992 and has an observation deck with information on its panels. Excellent panoramic views of the city and surroundings, including the nearby mountains. Location: Avenida de la Memoria 2; Hours: Tue-Sun: 9:30 am-8:00 pm; cost: 4 euros, reduced admission also available. From Plaza de España it's a 10-15 minute bus ride on line 2 to the Moncloa area. Look for the Triumphal Arch; then you'll see that the Tower just behind this huge arch.

Chapter 8

Museums and Artists

El Prado

Originally designed as a place for science, Maria Isabel encouraged her husband King Ferdinand VII to have it be a museum, and he made it one to store royal paintings. Opened in 1819, its collections include masterpieces of Spanish, Italian, Flemish, and French artists up to 1881. There are also outstanding sculptures and works of decorative arts. There's a great deal of Spanish history in its exhibits. The Prado played a key role in the history of art and has served to inspire many avant-garde painters of the last 150 years. It holds a special place in my heart for personal reasons. Location: Calle Alfonso XII number 28. Hours: Mon-Sat 10am-8pm; Sun and holidays 10am-7pm; Jan 6, Dec 24 and 31 10am-2pm; closed Jan 1, May 1, and Dec 25. General admission: 15 euros (about $16.), check days and times for free and reduced admissions.

Las Meninas by Velázquez

Velázquez in the Prado

Diego Rodríguez de Silva y Velázquez, (1599-1660), was the leading painter in the court of King Philip IV of Spain and Portugal, and of the Spanish Golden Age. He painted a multitude of portraits of the Spanish royal family and commoners, culminating in his masterpiece Las Meninas, a slice of royal court life which continues to be studied even today by students, scholars, and critics. His paintings influenced painters in the 1800s and 1900s, including Pablo Picasso and Salvador Dalí. Having given this brief look into his works, it's very fitting to see his statue in front of the main entrance to the Prado Museum, as many of his paintings are on exhibit inside. The statue was the idea of the Circle of Fine Arts, a non-profit organization, funded by the Society of Architects. Cast in bronze, it features a seated Velázquez, with his palette and brush resting on him. It was unveiled in 1899, as part of the festivities marking the 300th anniversary of the painter's birth.

Goya in the Prado

Francisco Goya (1746-1828) was one of the greatest painters and print-makers of his time.He bridges the "Old Masters" and the modern artists. He also influenced later well-known artists. His paintings, drawings, and engravings reflected historical upheavals of his day, in particular the horrors of the Napoleonic invasion in his series *The Disasters of War* (1810–14). Along the boulevard outside the front of the Prado Museum stands a statue of bronze, marble and granite of Goya.The sculptor who created it in 1902 was Mariano Benillure. Other statues dedicated to Goya are located near the Royal Palace and Retiro Park.

La Reina Sofia

This art center opened in 1990 with its headquarters in a building originally established as a hospital by King Philip II in the 1500s. With many additions and modifications from that time to this, it has become a modern Spanish museum for contemporary art. It serves multiple roles of exhibiting and expanding collections, educating the general public, holding international exhibitions, and offering training activities on its collections. In 1992 King Juan Carlos I and Queen Sofia inaugurated its permanent collection. Location: Calle de Santa Isabel 2; hours: Main Venue, Sabatini and Nouvel Building- Mon 10am-9pm, Tue closed, Wed-

Sat 10am-9pm, Sun 10am-2:30pm, Holidays - check schedule. General admission: 12 euros ($13.10).

Pablo Picasso in the Reina Sofia

Pablo Picasso (1881-1973) was born in Spain and died in France. He was constantly innovating art. He made over 20,000 paintings, sculptures, drawings, costumes and theater sets over his 93 year life span. He's celebrated as one of the most influential 20th century artists.One of his most famous paintings, a mural-sized work titled Guernica, has its own room in the Reina Sofia museum.It's regarded by many as the most moving painting depicting the horrors of war. Its title is from Guernica, a town in northern Spain of no military value, that was mercilessly bombed by German planes in support of Spain's General Franco. It was the first aerial saturation bombing of civilians.

Thyssen-Bornemisza

Known as the Thyssen, it's part of the "Golden Triangle of Art '' that also includes the Prado and the Reina Sofia. Baron Hans Heinrich Thyssen-Bornemisza and his father collected the works between the 1920s and 1980s; the museum opened in 1992. Its collection of over 1000 works of art span the 1300s through the more recent movements with works from the early Italians, German Renaissance, 19th century Americans, Impressionists, German Expressionists, and Russian Constructivists as the most represented. Location: Paseo del Prado 8. Hours: Monday: 12.00pm-4pm Free entry thanks to the sponsorship of Mastercard, Tue - Sun 10am-7pm; General Admission 13 euros ($14.20)

9

Chapter 9

Parks and Gardens

Retiro Park

Close to the Prado, created for the monarchy in the 1600s, it opened to the public in 1868.You can enjoy its boating lake, many fountains, statues, trees, amazing buildings, and plenty of activities such as roller-blading, fortune telling, yoga, puppet shows, and music; savor the foods offered at many stands, and stop by the stands with many other items for sale.Check out picnic tables and swings.You may want to try a tour on a segway offered through Tripadvisor. There's something for all ages. It's a designated UNESCO World Heritage Site. Location: Plaza de la Independencia 7. Hours: April to September 6am - 12 midnight; October to March 6am - 10pm. Park entrance is free. Boats can be rented for 45 minutes 10 am–2 pm and 3:15 pm–closing time, which varies by season. The cost is €6 ($6.55) Monday–Friday, €8 ($8.75) on weekends and holidays, and €2 ($2.20) per person for the solar-powered boats. People over 65 can get a 70% discount Monday–Friday before 2pm if they show their ID at the ticket office.

Casa de Campo

This is Madrid's largest park, almost 7 square miles. Created in the early 1500s for the royal family's use as their hunting grounds, its name means "Country House". It became a public park in the 1930s and is especially enjoyed by outdoors lovers who see it as more natural and biodiverse than other parks. You can just walk around, have picnics or enjoy the Zoo, its lake, a cable car ride, multi use pavilions and an amusement park that families especially like. The lake offers boat and kayak rentals; restaurants are around the lake. There is a large pool to cool you off. Location: Paseo de la Puerta del Angel 1; open 24 hours.

River Park (Madrid Río)

It began with an international ideas competition in 2005 on how to redevelop land along the Manzanares River for the public's benefit. It has running paths, fitness stations, beautiful bridges, game tables, music festivals, shows, picnic tables, a dog park, and a basketball court. There are great views of the Royal Palace and other landmarks. Both adults and children benefit from the wide variety of leisure and cultural activities. Location: Paseo de la Ermita del Santo 14-16; Open: 24 hours; free.

Sabatini Gardens

Built in the 1930s, the ornamental style of these unique gardens was an extension of the Royal Palace, located in front of the north face of the Palace. Several sculptures and geometric designs make them very beautiful. Dusk is when they are absolutely spectacular; it's one of the best places to watch the sunset.

10

Chapter 10

Historical Buildings

Convent of the Descalzas Reales

Founded in the mid 1500s by a daughter of King Charles V it's also called the "Monastery of the Royal Discalced" (those who wore sandals or went barefoot). It traditionally was open to young widowed or spinster noblewomen who each brought a dowry.With all the dowries and other support, it became one of the richest convents and eventually fell into poverty. In 1960 they were granted a special dispensation to open as a museum. Not only does their collection include priceless art masterpieces and tapestries, but also rare portraits of royal children. Location: Paseo de las Descalzas 3; cost: 8 euros ($8.77 US), free for certain groups. Hours:Tue-Sat 10-2pm and 4-6:30pm, Sun and holidays 10:00am-3:00pm.

Cervantes' Residence

Miguel de Cervantes (1547-1616) - full name Miguel de Cervantes Saavedra- was the most famous Spanish author of Spain's Golden Age (1500s and 1600s). One of his best-known books was Don Quixote of the Mancha; the main characters of Don Quixote and his servant Sancho are immortalized in a monument to Cervantes on the Plaza de España. A statue of Cervantes forms another part of that monument. His house was demolished so there's only a bust of Cervantes and an inscription on the face of the building to commemorate him. Location: Calle de Léon 7. He's buried in a nearby convent. He and Shakespeare died almost on the same day in 1616.

Lope de Vega's House/Museum

Lope de Vega (1562-1635) - full name Lope de Félix de Vega Carpio- is considered the modernizer of comedy and the true innovator of Spanish theater from Spain's Golden Age (1500s-1600s). He created over 1500 plays and 3000 poems. He and Cervantes were contemporaries and rivals. Oddly, his house which later became a museum was on Cervantes St. He lived in it until he died in 1635. Some of his paintings, art, books, and furniture were donated by one of his daughters. A monument to him is near the Royal Palace.

Location: Calle de Cervantes 11; note: Although the garden and temporary exhibition can be visited without prior booking, the museum can only be seen on a 35-minute guided tour which must be booked in advance.

Atocha Station (original part)

This is Madrid's first train station. The original part of the station opened in 1892. The architecture resembles that of a museum. The only hint that it's not is the clock on the outside. Its tracks were removed in 1992, and this old part of the station was converted into a tropical garden with bars and restaurants, which is a relaxing place to visit or to wait for someone's train to arrive.

11

Chapter 11

Monuments and Statues

Plaza de Cibeles

This square is a landmark and an important symbol of Madrid, located at the juncture of Alcalá St, Prado Blvd, and Recoletos Blvd. In its center is the fountain of the goddess Cybele (Cibeles) who was worshiped in ancient Greece and Rome. She is seated on her chariot which is pulled by two lions. It was constructed in the 1780s. Interestingly, the Royal Madrid Soccer team adopted this fountain, and their fans often celebrate successful games in it. The most prominent building on this square is the Communications Palace. Though it resembles a cathedral, it was built in 1909 as the postal service headquarters.In 2007 it became Madrid's City Hall.

Puerta de Alcalá

A triumphal arch in the Neoclassic style, it's the first of its type constructed after the days of the Roman Empire. It was once the main entrance gate to the city. King Charles II commissioned it, and Italian architect Francesco Sabatini had it built in 1778. (The king was said not to have been at all impressed by the gate he saw upon his initial arrival in 1759. Over time he and his subjects got along quite well, as he was nicknamed the Best Mayor of Madrid.) It is located next to Retiro Park, in the middle of Independence Square, on Madrid's longest street, known as Alcalá. If you follow Alcalá in one direction you'll end up in the Puerta del Sol.Going in the opposite direction you'll reach the city of Alcalá de Henares, the hometown of Miguel de Cervantes, Spain's Golden Age author of Don Quixote.

Look at the gate from each side, and you'll see different designs on each. The one that looks towards the center of the city has sculptures of war trophies such as weapons, flags, and helmets; its three rounded arches are decorated with a lion's head. On the side that travelers would first see as they arrived are more ornate decorations, and it features the royal coat of arms held up by a representation of Fame, assisted by a child. Along the top of the gate, you'll notice the figures of four children representing the cardinal virtues: fortitude, justice, temperance and prudence.

12

Chapter 12

Food and Entertainment

One of the most fun activities is to go tapa bar hopping. You'll find Madrileños going throughout the evening and later. Dinner is around 10 pm and then on to clubs to dance or to theaters to see a show. Everyone has their favorite tapa bars, cafes, and restaurants. Think of tapas as appetizers, usually accompanied by a small glass of wine or draft beer. People usually stand at the bar rather than sit at a table; you pay less if you stand. Most of the tapa bars and restaurants are in the areas around Sol and Plaza Mayor. I've included walking directions so you can see more of Madrid while you're getting where you want to go.

Tapa Bars

The most well-known street for tapa bars in Calle Cava Baja. Just follow Calle Cuchilleros off the Plaza Mayor. It becomes Calle Cava Baja after passing the Plaza Puerta Cerrada. You'll find over 40 bars. One of my favorite tapas is gambas al ajillo (garlic shrimp). Others are tortilla española (Spanish tortilla is really an omelet of potatoes and eggs) and jamón Serrano (special Spanish ham). Try as many as you can. Your taste buds will thank you.

San Miguel Market

Designed by Eiffel, the same engineer of Paris' Eiffel Tower, it was built around 1916. It was almost demolished but rescued as a designated historic building. It's an open air food market with several tapa bars and restaurants. It's easy to find on the Plaza de San Miguel, just off the Plaza Mayor along the Calle Cuchilleros.

El MiniBar

Here's a good place for tapas and dinner. Reservations are required. Located at Calle de los Paños 1. Hours: M-Th 10am-1am, F 10am-2:30am, Sat 12pm-2:30am, Sun 12pm-1am. It's about 7 minutes to walk from Sol: take Calle Arenal, left on C de las Hileras, slightly left on Plaza de Herradores, right on Calle del Bonetillo/Plaza de Herradores, continue on Costera de Santiago, and turn right onto Calle de los Paños. Phone: (34) 696 05 51 94.

Restaurants and Cafes

Casa Botín

According to the Guiness Book of World Records, this is the world's oldest restaurant, founded in 1725. Its notable specialties are suckling pig and lamb roasted in the Castilian style. Its entire menu offers the highest standard of traditional Madrid cuisine. Located at Calle Cuchilleros 17, which is one of the streets that leads out of the Plaza Mayor, it's open every day for lunch 1-4pm and dinner 8-11:30pm. Reservations required; main phone: (34) 91 366 42 17.

Taberna La Bola

La Bola has been serving traditional Spanish food for over a century. A typical Madrid dish offered here is *cocido madrileño* (Madrid stew). Located at Calle de la Bola 5. Hours: Sun-W 1-4pm; Th,F, Sat 12pm-9:30pm; prices: $34-55 US. Reservations are required. Directions from the Royal Palace area: about a 7 minute walk; go to the Plaza de Oriente, turn right onto Calle de San Quintín, go left onto Plaza de la Encarnación, and continue onto Calle de la Bola. Phone: (34) 915 47 69 30.

Churrería Chocolatería 1902

This long-time family run restaurant is famous for its churros and other pastries along with chocolate. You must try chocolate with churros; it's a luscious breakfast treat.Located at Calle de San Martín 2 with daily hours of 7am-12am. Prices range from $1.25 to $12 US. It's a 5 minute walk from Sol via Calle Arenal and taking a right a few blocks later onto Calle de San Martín. Phone: (34) 915 22 57 37.

La Mallorquina

Since 1894, La Mallorquina has been known for its amazing pastries and cakes. It also has a full menu restaurant on the second floor. It's at the western end of the Puerta del Sol number 8. Be sure to stop into this very popular spot. Phone: (34) 915 21 12 01.

Casa Mingo

This restaurant is considered authentically Madrid, as it offers classic fare along with its well-known cider made on the premises and its wonderful roasted chicken.It opened in 1888 and is near Plaza de España at Paseo de la Florida 34. Hours are every day 11 am-midnight; prices range from around $11 to $40 US per person, with the average around $24 US. You can get there from Plaza de España in about 10 minutes: take bus 46 in the direction of Moncloa and get off at the San Antonio de la Florida stop. Look for it about 200 feet away. Phone: (34) 91 547 79 18.

Brunchit Malasaña

Each Brunchit is unique. This one, located at Calle Noviciado 12, offers international and Mediterranean cuisine, has a children's menu, is vegetarian friendly with gluten free options, and has been highly rated by Tripadvisor reviewers. Hours: M-F 9am-4pm, Sa-Su 9am-4:30pm, for breakfast, lunch or brunch. Price range: $3-33 US. Directions from the Hotel Riu at the Plaza de España: go along Calle San Leonardo by the hotel, cross Calle San Bernardino, continuing along Calle Juan Dios, turn right onto Trva. del Conde Duque, cross over the Calle de Amaniel and continue onto Calle del Noviciado to number 12. Phone: (34) 911 08 94 46.

Donde Monica

Located away from the previous restaurants at Calle Padilla 3, near the corner of Padilla and Calle Serrano, is this cozy restaurant with a variety of dishes to enjoy inside or outdoors. Vegetarian and vegan options are available. Open M-F 9am-midnight, Sa 12:30 pm-midnight and Su 12pm-5pm; prices $33-$44 US. Directions from Plaza Cibeles: take bus line 27 in the direction of Plaza de Castilla; get off at the 4th stop which is Paseo de la Castellana at Rubén Darío. Cross over to Calle Serrano and go one block south (back down toward Cibeles) to the Calle de Padilla and go left to number 3.Phone: (34) 915 77 76 57.

Casa Dani

Everyone is urged to order (and glad they ate) Casa Dani's traditional Spanish omelet (tortilla española). This dish can be served hot or cold at any time of day, a slice or the whole thing. You can also taste other traditional Spanish foods here. What's unusual is that this restaurant is located inside a 19th century market, the Mercado de la Paz. It's at Calle de Ayala 28. Their sign is outside where they have a terrace next to the market, while the main part is inside, which can be confusing. Hours are M-F 6:30am-7:30pm and Sa 6:30am-4pm. Price range is about $12-22US. If you've already visited Donde Monica, you can get to Casa Dani in about 7 minutes by walking east on Calle Padilla to Calle de Claudio Cuello, taking a right onto Claudio Cuello, going 3 long blocks to Calle de Ayala, and turning left onto Ayala. The market is on your right before you get to Calle Lagasca. Phone: (34) 915 755 925.

More to try

Check out: https://www.tripadvisor.com/Restaurants-g187514-Madrid.html or https://www.eater.com/maps/best-madrid-restaurants-38

Flamenco

A flamenco group in an open air setting: dancer, guitarist, singer, and drummer

Corral de la Morería

It's a restaurant and the only flamenco *tablao* in Madrid to receive many national and international awards and a Michelin star; located at Calle de la Morería 17 with shows Tu-Su at 8pm, 8:30pm, 9 and 9:30 pm.prices start around $44US per person, depending on whether you go for dinner and a show, dinner only, and which show you choose. It's about a 7 minute walk from the Royal Palace: go to Calle de Bailén and turn right (south); continue past the major street of Calle de Segovia; turn right onto the Calle de la Morería and go to number 17. Main phone numbers: (34) 913 651 137 and (34) 91 365 84 46; reservations needed. *¡Diviértanse!*

Torres Bermejas

You can enjoy dinner and a renowned flamenco show here. It's unique because its rooms are reproductions of the historic site with the same name found in Spain's southern city of Granada. Located at Calle Mesonero Romanos 11; open daily; M-F shows at 5pm, 7pm and 11pm; Sa-Su at 3 pm, 5pm, 7pm and 11 pm. From Puerta de Sol a 5 minute walk: take Calle del Carmen from Sol until you come to Calle de Mesonero Romanos and turn right; continue to number 11. Cost: dinner and a show starts at $40-55 US per person. Reservations needed; main phone number: (34) 690 90 93 58. *¡Olé!*

Family Friendly Places

Casa de Campo

Location: Paseo de la Puerta del Angel 1; open 24 hours: amusement park, playground, cable car, and zoo.For details see earlier chapter on Parks and Gardens.

Retiro Park

For details see earlier chapter on Parks and Gardens.

Wax Museum

A super place to visit with children. It combines history - over 450 people represented from different time periods- and occupations: famous athletes, politicians, and celebrities.especially for young people are characters such as Pocoyo, Elly and Duck, E.T. and Buzz Lightyear. One of its most successful galleries with the adults is the Wax Horror Experience, focusing on horror films with figures like Hannibal Lecter. There's also a Horror Train ride, which takes you from Jurassic Park to the Galactic Tavern and has several surprises.It's open daily 11am-8 pm and costs $20.63 through various websites. It's located at Plaza de Colón 1. From Plaza de Cibeles take bus line 27 and get off at Plaza de Colón stop; use the crosswalk to cross the street and look for the entrance.

Railway Museum

Take a trip through the history of train travel in Madrid; its restaurant has food from all over Spain. This museum is in the former Delicias station at Paseo de las Delicias 61. In addition to all the trains, it houses the Historical Archives and Railway and Newspaper Libraries. Hours: June-Sept daily 10am-3pm; Oct-May M-F 9:30am-3 pm, Sa 10am-7pm,

Su 10am–3pm; general admission is $7.60, reduced for various groups, just show your ID. The easiest way to get there is by metro line 3 from Sol to Delicias.

La Mar de Letras

Children's bookstore that's located near the Royal Palace and specializes in books for young children and youth. Its main purpose is to encourage them to enjoy reading from an early age. It has won the National Bookseller Award.Address: Calle de Santiago 18; hours: Tu– F 10am–8pm, Sa 10am–2pm, Su–M closed. From Palacio Real it's a 4 minute walk: go south on Calle de Bailén toward Calle de la Requena, left onto Calle de la Requena, slight right onto Plaza de Ramales, continue onto Calle de Santiago, turn left at Plaza de Santiago/Calle de Santiago, continue to number 18.

Shopping

El Corte Inglés

A department store chain with stores throughout the city; some have supermarkets on the lowest level. One is near Sol, another is on Calle Princesa, and yet another is close to the Santiago Bernabéu Stadium.

Galerías Preciados

Like El Corte Inglés it's a department store chain with stores throughout the city; the one between Puerta del Sol and the Gran Via has an observation deck on the top floor along with multiple bars and cafes.

Galerías Canalejas

This is a high end shopping and dining center near Plaza Cibeles that occupies seven monumental buildings with significant historical, architectural and cultural value from 1887 to the present. You may want to window shop around the complex, as it boasts of fashion, fine jewelry and accessories of very prestigious brands as well as more than 13 restaurants with specialties from different nations.

Gran Via / Callao

The entire street is a shopper's paradise that has lots of shops, theaters, and some hotels/hostels.

Puerta del Sol

There are many small shops or niche shops in and around the Puerta del Sol. Some examples include chocolate shops, rare books, mantillas, fans, and Toledo steel articles.

Sports

The favorite sport is soccer; here are the main home teams and their stadiums; plenty of rivalry exists between these teams and their fans:

Santiago Bernabéu Stadium

Home to the Royal Madrid team; completely renovated over the last few years; situated on the Paseo de la Castellana.

Wanda Metropolitano Stadium

Home of the Madrid Atlético team; located at Avenida de Luis Aragonés, 4; the old one was demolished a few years ago.

13

Chapter 13

Conclusion

That wraps up your 24 hour visit to begin getting acquainted with friendly and lively Madrid. I hope you've enjoyed reading this book as much as I have enjoyed creating it for you. May you return to explore more of Madrid!

Just one request: If you've found this book helpful or interesting, I'd appreciate it if you would leave a favorable review for it on Amazon. *¡Mil gracias!*

14

Chapter 14

Resources

"Almudena Cathedral." *Wikipedia*, 20 Feb. 2023, en.wikipedia.org/wiki/ Almudena_Cathedral.

"Architecture & Heritage | Galería Canalejas." *Galeriacanalejas.com*, www.galeriacanalejas.com/en/architecture-and-heritage/. Accessed 26 July 2024.

"Botín Restaurant | Centennial Restaurant | Guinness World Records." *Https://Botin.es/En/Home/*, botin.es/en/home/.

"Casa de Campo." *Turismo Madrid*, www.esmadrid.com/barrios-de-madrid/casa-campo. Accessed 26 July 2024.

"Casa Mingo | Roast Chicken Madrid." *Https://Www.casamingo.es/?Lang=En*, www.casamingo.es/?lang=en. Accessed 26 July 2024.

"El Retiro Park." *Madrid Tourisme*, 2019, www.esmadrid.com/en/ tourist-information/parque-del-retiro.

Falomir, Miguel. "Collection - Museo Nacional Del Prado." *Www.museodelprado.es*, www.museodelprado.es/en/the-collection.

"Faro de Moncloa." *Turismo Madrid*, www.esmadrid.com/en/tourist-information/faro-de-moncloa . Accessed 26 July 2024.

"Getting There - Official Atlético de Madrid Website." *Club Atlético de Madrid*, 23 July 2024, en.atleticodemadrid.com/atm/location-3. Accessed 26 July 2024.

"Home." *Casamuseolopedevega.org*casamuseolopedevega.org/en/home-en . Accessed 26 July 2024.

"Inicio." *Turismo Madrid*, 2020, www.esmadrid.com.

"La Mar de Letras." *Official Tourism Website*, www.esmadrid.com/compras/la-mar-de-letras . Accessed 26 July 2024.

"Lope de Vega House Museum." *Turismo Madrid*, www.esmadrid.com/en/tourist-information/casa-museo-lope-de-vega . Accessed 26 July 2024.

Mancebo, Ivanka Garcia. "The Madrid Railway Museum - Opening Hours Price and Location." *Www.introducingmadrid.com* , www.introducingmadrid.com/rail-museum. Accessed 26 July 2024.

Mercado San Miguel | Mercado. www.mercadodesanmiguel.es/ .

"Monument to Miguel de Cervantes." *Wikipedia*, 16 July 2024, en.wikipedia.org/wiki/Monument_to_Miguel_de_Cervantes . Accessed 26 July 2024.

"Parroquia de San Jerónimo El Real." *Www.parroquiasanjeronimoelreal.es* .

"Pastelería La Mallorquina Puerta Del Sol." , pastelerialamallorquina.es/tiendas/puerta-del-sol/ . Accessed 26 July 2024.

"Plaza Mayor." *Official Tourism Website*, 2018, www.esmadrid.com/informacion-turistica/plaza-mayor-madrid .

"Puerta de Alcalá." *Turismo Madrid*, www.esmadrid.com/en/tourist-information/puerta-de-alcala .

"Railway Museum." *Turismo Madrid*, www.esmadrid.com/en/tourist-information/museo-del-ferrocarril . Accessed 26 July 2024.

rcferegrino3@hotmail.com. "TOP Tapas in Madrid Sol and Where to

Eat Them." *Tapas Tour Madrid*, 7 Nov. 2021, www.tapastour.madrid/ tapas-madrid-sol/.

Accessed 26 July 2024.

"Royal Palace of Madrid." *Patrimonio Nacional*, 2020, www.patrimonionacional.es/en/visita/royal-palace-madrid.

"Sabatini Gardens." *Turismo Madrid*, www.esmadrid.com/en/tourist-information/jardines-de-sabatini.

Sandra. "Plaza de Cibeles." *Madrid Traveller*, 5 Mar. 2023, www.madrid-traveller.com/plaza-de-cibeles/.

Smith, Mark. "Madrid Atocha Station - a Short Guide." *Www.seat61.com*, www.seat61.com/stations/madrid-atocha.htm#Changing_trains_at_Atocha.

Accessed 26 July 2024.

"Tapa Tapa Arenal TT7." *TAPA TAPA RESTAURANT*, tapataparestaurant.com/reservas/tapa-tapa-arenal/. Accessed 26 July 2024.

"The World's Most Popular Urban Mobility App." *Moovit*, moovitapp.com.

"TripAdvisor: Consulta Opiniones, Compara Precios Y Reserva." *TripAdvisor*, 2013, www.tripadvisor.es/.

U.S. News & World Report. "20 Best Things to Do in Madrid | U.S. News Travel." *Usnews.com*, U.S. News & World Report, 26 Sept. 2019, travel.usnews.com/Madrid_Spain/Things_To_Do/.

"Velazquez - Google Search." *Www.google.com*, www.google.com/search?gs_ssp=eJzj4tDP1TfItjSqNGD04ixLzUmsKixNrQIAQnUGyA& q=velazquez&rlz=1C1NHXL_enUS913US913&oq=vel. Accessed 26 July 2024.

Wikipedia Contributors. "Statue of Velázquez (Madrid)." *Wikipedia*, Wikimedia Foundation, 13 Aug. 2023, en.wikipedia.org/wiki/Statue_of_Vel%C3%A1zquez_(Madrid). Accessed 26 July 2024.

Made in the USA
Las Vegas, NV
21 October 2024

10238412R00036